AF270504

JOBS WITH ANIMALS

BY TAMMY GAGNE

Core Library

An Imprint of Abdo Publishing
abdobooks.com

Cover image: Dog groomers are responsible for bathing dogs and giving them haircuts.

abdobooks.com

Printed in China.
052023
092023

Cover Photo: Oleksandr Rupeta/NurPhoto/Getty Images
Interior Photos: iStockphoto, 4–5, 42 (top); Joshua Lott/The Washington Post/Getty Images, 7; Nick Schnelle/
The Columbia Daily Tribune/AP Images, 10; JW Design/Shutterstock Images, 12–13; David McKeown/Standard-
Speaker/AP Images, 15, 42 (middle); Red Line Editorial, 16, 25; Aaron Chown/PA Images/Getty Images, 19, 43
(middle), 45; Anthony Devlin/Getty Images News/Getty Images, 20; Lillian Suwanrumpha/AFP/Getty Images,
22–23; Bestami Bodruk/Anadolu Agency/Getty Images, 27; Brandon Bell/Getty Images News/Getty Images,
29, 43 (top middle); Jens Büttner/picture alliance/Getty Images, 32–33, 43 (bottom middle); Michael Macor/
The San Francisco Chronicle/Hearst Newspapers/Getty Images, 35; Thomas A. Ferrara/Newsday RM/Getty
Images, 38; Deaan Vivier/Beeld/Gallo Images/Getty Images, 40; Linda Davidson/The Washington Post/Getty
Images, 42 (top middle); Dalibor Gluck/CTK/AP Images, 42 (bottom middle); aldomurillo/E+/Getty Images,
42 (bottom); Paul Chinn/The San Francisco Chronicle/Hearst Newspapers/Getty Images, 43 (top); Jeff
Roberson/AP Images, 43 (bottom)

Editor: Laura Stickney
Series Designer: Katharine Hale

Library of Congress Control Number: 2022949096

Publisher's Cataloging-in-Publication Data

Names: Gagne, Tammy, author.
Title: Jobs with animals / by Tammy Gagne
Description: Minneapolis, Minnesota: Abdo Publishing Company, 2024 | Series: Industry jobs | Includes online
    resources and index.
Identifiers: ISBN 9781098290917 (lib. bdg.) | ISBN 9781098277093 (ebook)
Subjects: LCSH: Occupations--Juvenile literature. | Animal husbandry--Biography--Juvenile literature. |
    Zoology--Biography--Juvenile literature.
Classification: DDC 590.23--dc23

CONTENTS

CHAPTER ONE
A Day at the Animal Shelter **4**

CHAPTER TWO
Jobs in Animal Facilities **12**

CHAPTER THREE
Jobs in Animal Health **22**

CHAPTER FOUR
Jobs in Animal Training **32**

Job List **42**

Stop and Think **44**

Glossary **46**

Online Resources **47**

Learn More **47**

Index **48**

About the Author **48**

A DAY AT THE ANIMAL SHELTER

Kelsey's day at the animal shelter started with paperwork. Every morning, she gathered the adoption applications from the previous afternoon. It was her job to decide which applicants could adopt animals. She felt hopeful when she saw how many applications there were. Many people were interested in adopting a pet from the shelter. Surely there were some wonderful potential owners within the stack.

Animal adoption counselors help match people with pets who need homes. They guide new owners through the adoption process.

Kelsey loved her job as an adoption counselor. But it wasn't always easy to find the best owners for dogs and cats in the facility. Puppies and kittens almost always found homes first. Young adult animals were also popular. Many people wanted to adopt animals that were already housetrained. These pets had already learned to go to the bathroom outdoors or in litter boxes.

But fewer people wanted senior pets. These animals were often less playful and had already lived most of

their lives. Some people even abandoned pets at the shelter because they were old.

But Kelsey felt positive about today. Scott and Lisa were a young couple whom Kelsey had met the day before. They had applied to adopt Ginger, a Labrador retriever mix who had been at the shelter for nearly six months. Many visitors had walked by Ginger and smiled at the large seven-year-old dog. But no one ever considered adopting her until yesterday. Scott and Lisa were drawn to Ginger instantly. Kelsey observed all three of them when they moved to the meeting room, where potential owners interacted with animals. Kelsey could tell from Ginger's wagging tail and relaxed posture that she liked Scott and Lisa.

But Kelsey had to make sure that the couple was a good fit for Ginger. Adopting a pet is a big responsibility. Kelsey wanted to give each animal the best chance of finding a home that would keep it for the rest of its life. Kelsey looked over the couple's responses to the application questions. They had owned a Labrador retriever before. He had died recently at age 11. Their home had a fenced yard. They listed their veterinarian and several friends as references. These people assured the shelter that Scott and Lisa were responsible people who would make good pet owners.

Everything looked great. Kelsey called Scott and Lisa to tell them the good news. They could now make plans to pay the adoption fee and pick up their new pet. Kelsey loved overseeing this stage of the adoption process. It always warmed her heart to see a pet go home with its new family.

WORKING WITH ANIMALS

Being an adoption counselor is just one option for people who want to work with animals. Animal lovers can choose from many careers. People who enjoy math and science may become veterinarians, who are experts in animal health. People who excel in science can become biologists. These scientists study wild animals to help them thrive in their natural habitats.

Other people may be drawn to more creative jobs, such as grooming or

JOB SHADOWING AND VOLUNTEERING

Young people interested in working with animals can try job shadowing. This involves observing a person at work. Shadowing is a great way to learn more about a job. Some workplaces, such as animal shelters, also allow young people to volunteer at their facilities. Older kids might help walk dogs. Younger kids might cuddle cats and other small animals. By volunteering, animal lovers can make a difference in animals' lives while seeing what it is like to work at a shelter.

Zoologists and wildlife biologists may locate animals in the wild for testing. This might involve taking blood samples, checking for diseases, or tagging animals.

dog training. These careers do not require as much education as jobs in medicine or science. But they still require training and practice. Dog trainers might show owners how to teach their pets manners or tricks.

Other trainers work with service dogs, who perform important tasks for people with disabilities.

Working with animals can be fun and rewarding, but it's also a lot of hard work. People must put time and effort into a career with animals. This way, they can make a difference in the lives of both animals and humans.

EXPLORE ONLINE

Chapter One discusses working with animals. The article at the website below explores different animal-related careers. How is the information from the website the same as the information in Chapter One? What new information did you learn from the website?

SO, YOU WANT TO WORK WITH ANIMALS

abdocorelibrary.com/jobs-with-animals

JOBS IN ANIMAL FACILITIES

Some animal lovers find jobs at animal shelters and rescue organizations. These facilities take in homeless or unwanted pets, such as dogs, cats, and birds. Shelters and rescues need many workers to care for these animals until they are adopted by new owners. All animals must be fed daily. Dogs must be walked. Litter boxes, kennels, and towels must be cleaned. Animals also need regular attention and play time. Some shelter workers bathe pets, too.

Animal shelter workers make sure animals receive food, water, and exercise. They may keep track of animals' medications.

FOCUSING THEIR EFFORTS

Some people may want a career that helps a particular animal breed or species. For example, dog lovers may start a rescue for German shepherds, Labrador retrievers, or pit bulls. These dogs are commonly surrendered to animal shelters. Biologists may want to work specifically with amphibians, such as frogs, toads, or salamanders. Many amphibian species are endangered. Humans can make a difference by getting involved in the rescue and conservation of these species.

Working at an animal shelter often requires on-the-job training. Workers must learn the various steps involved in caring for animals. Although shelter workers need training, they do not need a high school diploma or college degree. But they should have genuine affection for animals. This can make parts of the job very difficult emotionally.

For example, most workers feel sad when they see animals who have been mistreated. Shelter workers must be caring and gentle. But they must control their

emotions and focus on what is best for the animals. Shelter workers should also be organized and have good time management skills. They must be able to work unsupervised.

Shelter workers spend a lot of time with animals in their care. It can be easy to get attached to the animals. Workers might miss animals who get adopted. But seeing animals go home with good families makes the job a rewarding experience. Each person who cares for a homeless pet makes a difference in that animal's life.

SAVING WILD ANIMALS

Pets aren't the only animals that need help from humans. Wild animals might become sick or injured.

BREAKDOWN OF DAILY TASKS FOR A WILDLIFE REHABILITATOR

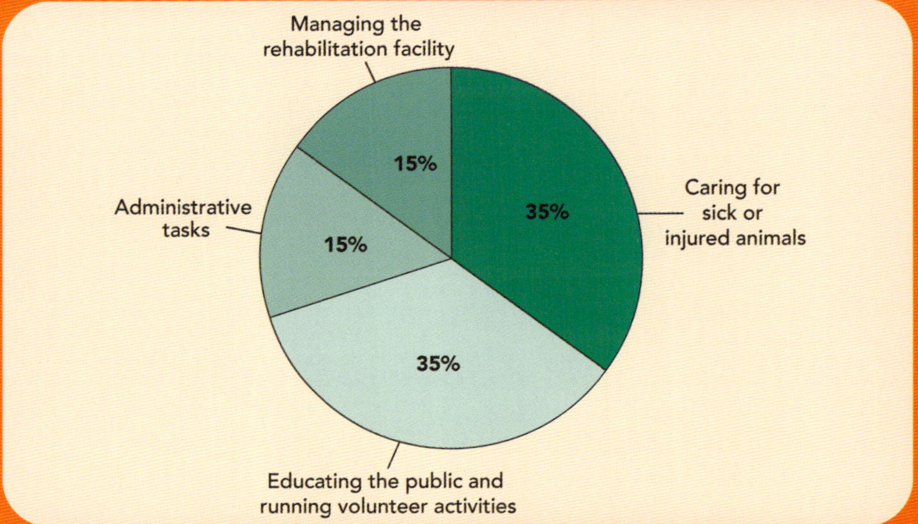

Most wildlife rehabilitators do more than care for sick or injured animals. They must divide their time between several tasks. How do you think educating the public impacts animals? Why is this part of a rehabilitator's job important?

Young animals are sometimes orphaned in the wild. To survive, these animals often need help from experienced caregivers. Wildlife rehabilitators perform this important work.

Rehabilitators do not need a college education. But college degrees in biology or animal science are helpful. People can earn bachelor's, associate's, and other advanced degrees in the field. Rehabilitators often learn how to care for animals by volunteering at wildlife rehabilitation centers or zoos. All rehabilitators must be certified by the International Wildlife Rehabilitation Council. To get certified, all rehabilitators must pass a written test. They must renew their certification every two years.

Wildlife rehabilitators need a strong understanding

of animal health and behavior. This often comes from a natural curiosity about wildlife. Most importantly, they understand that wild animals differ from pets. Unlike shelter workers, rehabilitators must meet an animal's needs without giving it too much personal attention. They must remember that the goal is for the animal to live on its own. Teaching animals to depend on humans can make it harder for them to return to the wild.

Much of a rehabilitator's work involves daily chores such as cleaning cages and feeding animals. If an animal is hurt, rehabilitators may need to treat its wounds and change bandages. Sometimes wild animals need veterinary care. In these situations, rehabilitators work with a veterinarian who treats that species.

Sometimes animals are unable to return to the wild. They may not fully recover from injuries. If an animal is unable to live on its own, a rehabilitator must find a place for it to live. Zoos or animal sanctuaries often take in these animals. The animals can live the rest of their lives receiving care in the safety of these facilities.

Zookeepers may be responsible for preparing an animal's food and keeping track of its diet. Some zookeepers specialize in working with specific types of animals.

WORKING AT ZOOS

Some jobs with animals involve working at zoos. Many people are needed to run a zoo. Zoo workers include zookeepers, aquarists, and zoologists. Zookeepers take care of animals' basic needs. They are responsible for feeding animals and keeping their enclosures clean. Aquarists perform this type of care for fish and other aquatic zoo animals. Zookeepers and aquarists must have a passion for animals and conservation. They must pay close attention to animals under their care and understand different animals' needs. They often work up close with animals. These jobs do not always require

a diploma. But it is becoming more common for zoos to hire people with college degrees in zoology.

Zoologists study animal health and behavior. They conduct experiments, do research, and collect data about wild animals. This helps them learn about animal habitats, diseases, invasive species, and more. Some zoologists study specific animals, such as reptiles or birds. They may work outdoors, in labs, or in offices. This work requires strong observational and outdoor skills, along with knowledge of biology and math. Most entry-level zoologist positions require a bachelor's degree, but advanced degrees may also be needed.

STRAIGHT TO THE
SOURCE

Neda Othman studied animal biology at the University of California, Davis School of Veterinary Medicine. She advises people interested in working with wildlife to attend a university:

> *If you are hoping to work with wildlife, a research university may be your best bet. Many research institutions conduct a myriad of studies on captive and free-ranging wildlife to answer many important questions and strongly encourage students to get involved with research projects. Some of these projects may even involve international work with animals—I know college students who have worked on projects in Africa with gorillas, in South America with sea turtles, and in Italy with feral swine!*

Source: Neda Othman. "Ultimate Guide to Wildlife Conservation Jobs." *Ecology Project International*, 7 July 2020, ecologyproject.org. Accessed 9 Dec. 2022.

WHAT'S THE BIG IDEA?

Take a close look at this passage. Why does Othman suggest that people attend a university if they are interested in working with wildlife? What evidence does she offer to support her opinion?

JOBS IN ANIMAL HEALTH

Some animal-related jobs involve helping animals look and feel their best. Dog and cat owners must perform many chores to keep their pets happy and healthy. Tasks such as bathing, cleaning ears, and trimming toenails are things that many pets need done regularly. Some owners lack the skills, patience, or time to perform these tasks themselves. These owners hire professionals to groom their pets.

Groomers may need to detangle a pet's hair or remove matted fur while grooming. They must also check the pet for any skin problems.

23

Being groomed by a stranger can make animals feel anxious or excited. Groomers help calm pets through good communication and a positive attitude. Some pets resist the grooming process by wiggling. This makes it challenging for groomers to trim hair neatly and use sharp tools. Because of this, it's helpful for groomers to have steady hands. Groomers do not have to be especially tall or strong, but they must be able to lift larger pets. Groomers also spend many hours on their feet.

SALARIES OF VETERINARY MEDICINE JOBS

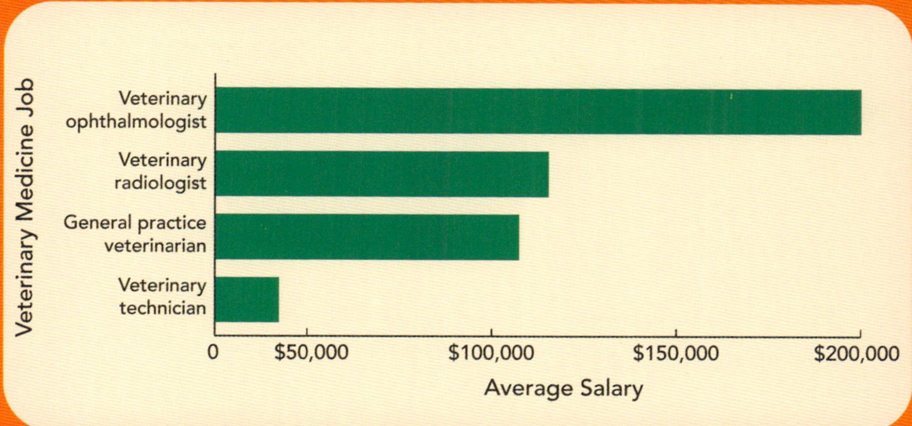

People working in veterinary medicine earn a wide range of salaries. In 2021, veterinary ophthalmologists made the most money. These doctors specialize in eye health. They must go to school for about three years longer than other vets. Why do you think people might choose a career that requires so much time and education?

Groomers may work for grooming salons, boarding kennels, or veterinary clinics. Many pet supply stores also offer grooming services. Other groomers run their own businesses. Groomers who book their own appointments must have good organization skills to stay on schedule. They may hire office staff to help.

Learning to groom different dog and cat breeds requires time and practice. It can take between a few weeks and a few months to learn the skills needed for this work. In most areas, pet groomers do not need licensing or certification. But attending a grooming school or passing the National Dog Groomers Association of America exam helps many groomers find jobs. Some grooming businesses also offer apprenticeships. This is when an experienced groomer spends extensive time teaching and training a person interested in entering the profession.

VETERINARY CARE

To keep pets healthy, owners must take them to a veterinary hospital for regular checkups. Injured or ill pets may also need to visit one of these facilities. People who work at veterinary hospitals include office workers, veterinary technicians, and veterinarians.

The first people most pet owners see at a veterinary hospital are office workers, such as receptionists.

Vet techs may help veterinarians by restraining animals during exams and preparing lab tests. Some vet techs specialize in working with wild animals at zoo hospitals.

These people answer phones, make appointments, greet clients, and handle billing and filing. Veterinary office workers often greet animals and hand out treats. They must be good with people and have excellent organization skills. Since they often work amidst noisy barks and meows, office workers must also be able to handle distractions.

Veterinary technicians, or vet techs, also work at veterinary hospitals. These workers bring pets

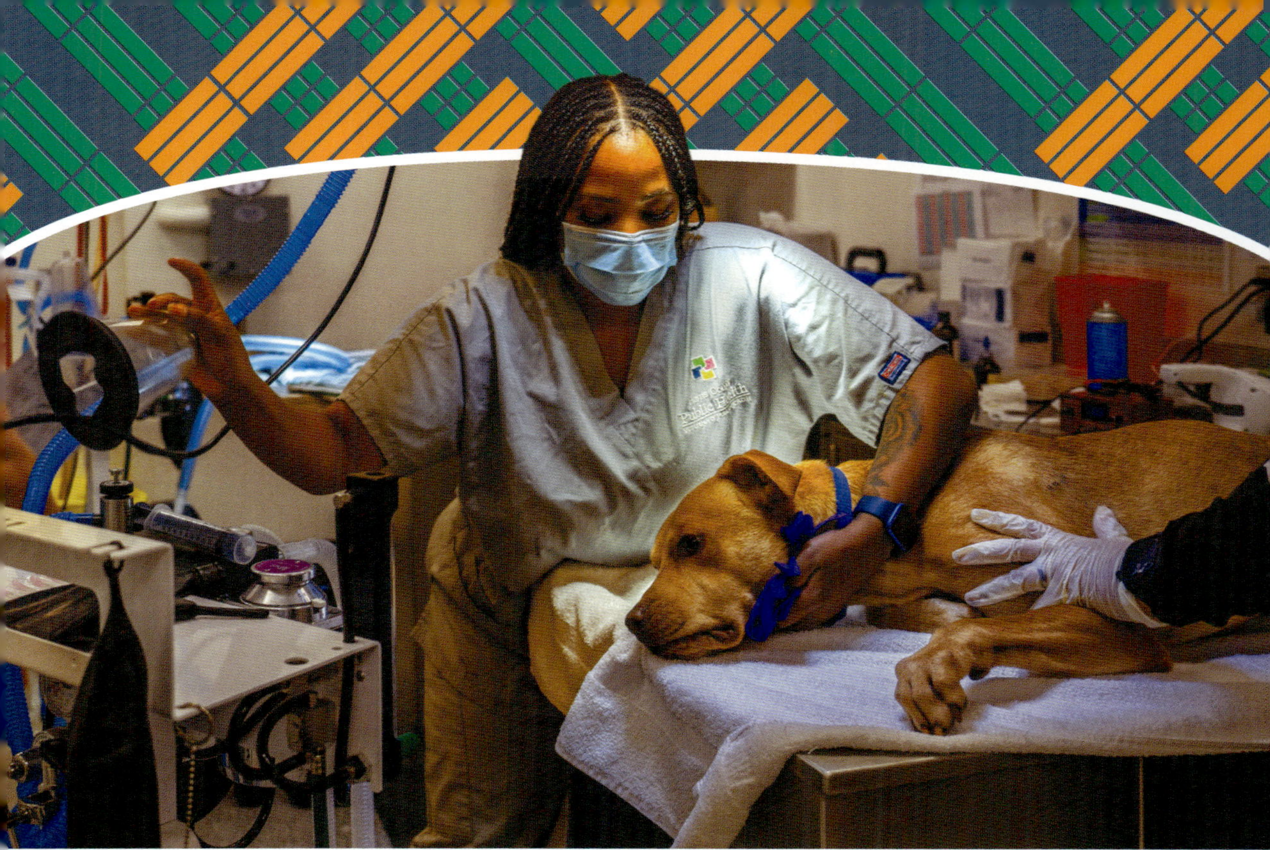

Vets must know how to use medical equipment and perform health exams correctly. Some vets specialize in specific areas of veterinary medicine, such as surgery.

and owners to the exam room. Before the exam, vet techs ask pet owners questions about their animals' health and record the answers. Then they stay for the veterinary exam, helping the veterinarian. This job often requires an associate's degree in veterinary technology, which takes about two years to earn. Many states also require vet techs to get a license. They must pass a test to become licensed.

Veterinarians, or vets, perform health exams and treat pets at veterinary hospitals. Most vets work with domesticated animals, such as dogs, cats, and horses. But some vets specialize in treating wildlife. These veterinarians may work at rehabilitation centers or zoos. Both types of vets must earn a bachelor's degree and then graduate from veterinary school. The doctor of veterinary medicine (DVM) degree takes about four years to earn. Before they can work as veterinarians, DVM graduates must also become licensed in their state.

Vets must be comfortable working closely with animals. They give pets vaccines to prevent common illnesses and medication to treat health problems. They may perform surgery on animals, too. Some operations fix health problems. Others prevent pets from producing offspring. Vets also advise pet owners about how to keep their pets healthy. For this reason, vets must have strong communication skills.

STRAIGHT TO THE
SOURCE

In an article for Medium, dog groomer Jess Rona shared that many of her friends think being a groomer is all fun. While Rona enjoys her job, she explained that it isn't as easy as many people imagine:

Groomers don't get to play with dogs all day. Don't get me wrong, after a dog has been groomed and they are all done, I tell them they're pretty and give them a kiss and a high five, but most of my day is dealing with dogs who avoid me at every turn.

I think it's safe to say no dog likes getting his nails trimmed, or ears cleaned. I don't blame them, I don't like it either. And that's the approach I take when grooming pups, I communicate to them that I know they don't like it, and I'm grateful to them for putting up with me.

Source: Jess Rona. "How to Have a Career as a Dog Groomer." Medium, 30 June 2018, medium.com. Accessed 9 Dec. 2022.

BACK IT UP

The author of this passage is using evidence to support a point. Write a paragraph describing the point the author is making. Then write down two or three pieces of evidence the author uses to make the point.

JOBS IN ANIMAL TRAINING

One of the most important things people can do for their pets is teach them proper behavior. Dogs that know basic obedience skills are welcome in many public places. Well-behaved dogs know how to walk calmly on a leash and focus on their owners. These dogs also greet people without jumping on them or mouthing them. But puppies are not born knowing these things. Owners must train them. Some owners might not know

Dog trainers must be able to work patiently with many different dog breeds. They identify a dog's problem behaviors and create training plans.

where to begin with this task. Professional animal trainers can help.

Some dog trainers teach owners how to train their own pets. These trainers may lead classes that owners attend with their pets. In this setting, trainers often teach basic commands, such as *sit*, *stay*, and *come*. Classes may meet once a week for several weeks. After watching a demonstration, owners practice the commands with their dogs during each session. The trainer assists them. Some trainers also offer advanced courses. For example, some owners compete in agility competitions with their dogs. In this canine sport, dogs race through obstacle courses made up of tunnels, jumps, and seesaws.

Other animal trainers work with horses. They train horses to make them rideable for people. Some horses kick, toss, or bite people who try to ride them. Trainers work with horses to stop these behaviors.

Some animal trainers work with racehorse riders to help prepare horses for races. They teach horses racing skills and make sure the animals stay healthy and fit.

Some horse owners compete in riding and jumping competitions with their animals. Trainers can help horses learn to perform these activities.

Other trainers use their skills to train animals for other types of performances, such as acting in movies or plays. Animals such as dogs are often used in films. But trainers may also work with birds, farm animals, or even tigers.

Animal trainers usually do not need

college educations. But they must spend a great deal of time learning animal training techniques. Some trainers have degrees in animal behavior, while others learn through hands-on practice. They may take classes, read articles, or watch online training videos. Trainers who teach pet owners must communicate well with others. They must be skilled at working with both owners and animals.

TRAINING WORKING ANIMALS

Some dogs have jobs of their own. Service dogs help people with disabilities or medical conditions. Police dogs work with police officers. Search and rescue dogs help find missing people. But before they can do any of these jobs, working dogs need extensive training.

Service dogs help disabled people live more independent lives. For example, a guide dog can help a person who is blind navigate through public places. Trainers teach these dogs how to lead humans safely along a city street. The animal wears a special harness

that the owner can hold. Service dogs that work with deaf people alert their owners when visitors knock on the door. Trainers practice the necessary tasks with these dogs until the animals can perform them without help. This process usually begins when the dog is just a puppy. It can take up to a year or more.

Police dogs and search and rescue dogs also require intense training. They use their sense of smell. Police dogs help officers find evidence of crimes.

Police dogs that work at airports sniff suitcases to detect any illegal materials that might be inside them. Some police dogs help capture criminals. Search and rescue dogs search for the scent of missing people. These dogs can follow a scent trail for miles, even if it has been days since the missing person was there.

Trainers generally work with dogs that show an early talent for scent work. They perform exercises with the dogs. This turns their natural abilities into highly specialized skills.

Training dogs for these professions takes time, effort, and skill. Most people who train working dogs start their careers as

CHANGE OF PLANS

Not all dogs have the intelligence or temperament required for certain jobs. Often, breeders will see an animal's potential for a career such as police work. But many dogs do not make it all the way to working in the field. When trainers realize that a dog isn't right for a certain job, they may recommend the animal for a different job. For example, some dogs start out training for police work and end up as service animals. Others become pets instead.

Dogs trained to work with police departments are often called K9s. Trainers help K9s practice identifying and tracing the scents of illegal materials, such as drugs or weapons.

regular dog trainers. They may then decide to learn

about training dogs for a particular profession. While

they do not need a college degree, some trainers take

classes in animal behavior. They may also earn degrees in this field.

People interested in jobs with animals have lots of options. Many careers offer rewarding work for people who enjoy spending time with dogs and other animals. Because each job is different, all animal lovers can find careers that are suited for them. They can use their skills to keep animals happy, healthy, and safe.

EXPLORE ONLINE

Chapter Four discusses service dogs that guide people who are blind. What is one of the main ideas of this chapter? What evidence is used to support this idea? Take a look at the website below. Does the information on the website support the main point of the chapter? Does it present new evidence?

GUIDE DOG TRAINING

abdocorelibrary.com/jobs-with-animals

JOB LIST

Animal adoption counselors review applications from potential pet owners. Counselors match them with available pets in need of homes.

Animal shelter workers perform duties such as cleaning, feeding, and walking animal shelter pets.

Wildlife rehabilitators care for orphaned, sick, or injured wild animals until they can return to the wild.

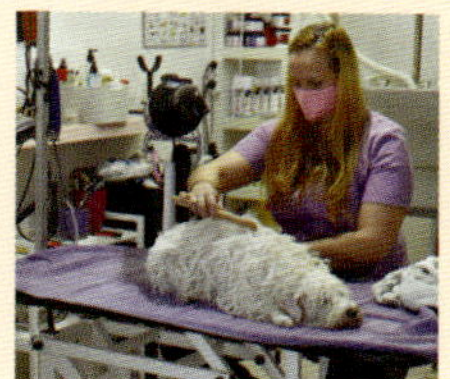

Groomers perform tasks such as bathing pets, trimming their fur, and cutting their nails. This helps keep pets healthy.

Veterinary hospital receptionists make appointments for pet owners, greet them upon arrival to the hospital, and handle billing.

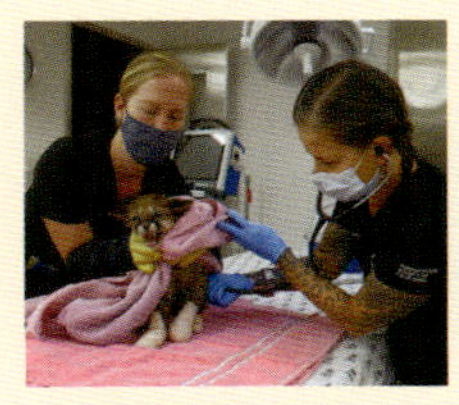

Veterinary technicians help veterinarians by gathering information from pet owners and assisting in the examination process.

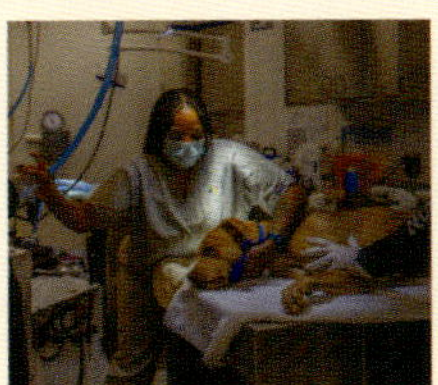

Veterinarians perform physical examinations to keep animals healthy. They treat sick pets and perform surgeries as needed.

Zookeepers take care of wild animals in zoos. They are responsible for feeding animals, monitoring their health, and keeping their enclosures clean.

Animal trainers train animals such as dogs or teach owners how to train their pets. Trainers may also work with horses, birds, and wild animals.

Service dog trainers train dogs to work with people who have disabilities or certain medical conditions.

STOP AND THINK

Take a Stand

Many animals are cared for in zoos. But some animal rights advocates think zoos are harmful. They believe zoos display wild animals for entertainment and cannot provide for their needs. Do you think zoos help or harm animals? Why?

Another View

This book talks about people who work for animal shelters. As you know, every source is different. Ask a librarian or another adult to help you find another source about jobs in animal shelters. Write a short essay comparing and contrasting the new source's point of view with that of this book's author. What is the point of view of each author? How are they similar and why? How are they different and why?

Tell the Tale

Chapter Three talks about how grooming keeps animals healthy. Imagine you are a dog groomer. Write 200 words about the tasks you perform each day. How do these tasks keep the dogs you groom in healthy condition?

Why Do I Care?

Maybe you own a pet or know someone who does. What would that pet's life be like without animal professionals? How do animal professionals help keep the pet healthy and safe?

GLOSSARY

conservation
the protection of an endangered living thing

counselor
a person who advises other people

domesticated
bred to have traits that make it easier for an animal to live alongside humans

euthanasia
the act of ending an animal's life painlessly to save it from suffering from a painful, incurable disease or injury

rehabilitator
a person who helps sick or injured people or animals return to health and activity

sanctuary
a place that provides wild animals with a safe home to live the remainder of their lives

stimulation
the act of inspiring interest, enthusiasm, or excitement

surrender
to give up or turn over ownership

temperament
the part of an animal's nature that affects its behavior

ONLINE RESOURCES

To learn more about jobs with animals, visit our free resource websites below.

Visit **abdocorelibrary.com** or scan this QR code for free Common Core resources for teachers and students, including vetted activities, multimedia, and booklinks, for deeper subject comprehension.

Visit **abdobooklinks.com** or scan this QR code for free additional online weblinks for further learning. These links are routinely monitored and updated to provide the most current information available.

LEARN MORE

Holmes, Parker. *K9 and Military Dogs*. Abdo, 2019.

Wild, Gabby, and Jennifer Szymanski. *Wild Vet Adventures*. National Geographic, 2020.

INDEX

animal adoption counselors, 5–8, 9

animal shelter workers, 5–8, 9, 13–15, 18

aquarists, 19–20

biology, 9, 14, 16, 20, 21

college degrees, 14, 16–17, 20, 29–30, 36–37, 40–41

conservation, 14, 17, 19

dog trainers, 10–11, 34, 36–41

groomers, 9, 23–26, 31

horse trainers, 34, 36

International Wildlife Rehabilitation Council, 17

National Dog Groomers Association of America, 26

police dogs, 37–39

search and rescue dogs, 37–39

service dogs, 11, 37–38, 39, 41

veterinarians, 8, 9, 18, 25, 26, 28, 29, 30

veterinary technicians, 25, 26, 28–29

wildlife rehabilitators, 16–18

zookeepers, 19–20

zoologists, 19–20

zoos, 17, 18, 19–20, 30

About the Author

Tammy Gagne has written hundreds of books for both adults and children. Some of her recent books are about paying for college and working as a graphic designer. She lives in northern New England with her husband, son, and dogs.